Safety Trip

poems by

Anna Papadopoulos

Finishing Line Press
Georgetown, Kentucky

Safety Trip

ACKNOWLEDGMENTS

Poems have appeared in the following periodicals, some in different forms:
Newtown Literary: "Sunday Mourning," "A Twenty-Three-Year-Old Dies Opening A
Door," "The Seed"
The Dillydoun Review: "The Immigrants' Children Grow Up," "The Last Day of Summer,"
"My Brother Tells His Story," "My Friends Are All Dying"
Second Chance Lit: "On Leaving Home"
Conestoga Zen Anthology: "Because I Don't Read Directions," "My Daughter Discovers
Her Face," "Zoom Freezes My Boss"
The Monterey Poetry Review: "Driving From My Childhood Home," "My First Adult
Furniture," "Snow Day with my Daughter," "A Warm February Day in New York."
The Closed Eye Open: "Cappadocia, Turkey"
Poetica Review: "Afghani Boy Whom I Will Never Know," "You'll Get The Tragic News,"
"He Takes His Children To The Site of His Victim's Remains"

This collection of poetry is dedicated to my family. My parents who taught me to be
curious. My brother, Nick, who's always had my back. My husband, Mike, for being my
emergency contact and designated driver. And my children, Michael, Elias, and Irene, my
greatest teachers. A special acknowledgment of gratitude for my longtime friend, Jeanne
Fama, for our many "safety trips."

The title of this collection, Safety Trip, is what my mother always says to us when we
embark on an adventure. Due to circumstances of World War II and the Greek Civil War
that followed, she never had a formal education and later emigrated to the United States
and learned English by listening to others; oftentimes, mishearing. And, with that, a
blessed adventure is forever a "safety trip."

Publisher: Leah Huete de Maines
Editor: Christen Kincaid
Cover Art: Anna Papadopoulos
Author Photo: Anna Papadopoulos
Cover Design: Elizabeth Maines McCleavy

Order online: www.finishinglinepress.com
also available on amazon.com

Author inquiries and mail orders:
Finishing Line Press
PO Box 1626
Georgetown, Kentucky 40324
USA

Contents

Leave

The story of life is quicker than the wink of an eye,
the story of love is hello and goodbye,
until we meet again.
Jimi Hendrix

Zoom Freezes His Face

It happens.
Mouth slightly opened
as if inhaling the room
and his face tilts
like a wall photo that has settled unevenly.
I lean in with confidence.

Blue-painted pinecones hang on his ceiling—
a crib mobile.
I imagine him gathering them for no reason:
I don't believe in frivolities,
he said, but now I know.

His features are engulfed, and I think,
how easy it is to disappear
to lose focus like this pixelated face;
Distorted sounds
escape from the speaker
like a man drowning.

Afghani

Zaki Anwari, a 17-year-old footballer with the Afghan national youth team, died after falling from a US air force plane on 16 August. He was attempting to flee his country after the Taliban seized control of districts across Afghanistan.
—*The New York Times, August 2021*

Footballer, son, brother, friend, boy
I will never know, now a speck hanging in
the Kabul air like a dot.

The US Air Force plane fuselage, an overpass
for your soul. The earth, a trampoline that can't hold you.

you. A firefly flashes in the sky, will freeze
time like those stars that we can't see.

Fires erupt, but not for the first or last time. Light
and warmth deceives with its grip, burns holes in the flesh.

Then, where is ideology, bombs, terror, the ocean
and that which it separates?

Where we can't see the falling child.

Cappadocia, Turkey

This message of longing,
petrified fossil on my soul,
Eastern Orthodox church domes
have eroded like my ancestors
who once lived here.

Fairy chimneys born of ash,
and ancient limestone caves
of coral remains. Sixty million years
in the making.

How can I crave what isn't mine?

What travels through my blood?
And what happened to the child my Yiayia buried?
Left among the evergreen perennials.

On Leaving Home

You won't return to the hand-woven sheep wool
blanket your mother made you. Or carry it,
for it will weigh you down and leave no room for water.

You will eat alone

You will travel where you won't know the word for bread
or work or love. Accept the staleness of what is given.
Say your last goodbye to your father on a faulty phone line
with other voices breaking through, as if, you were all
channeled to a simultaneous seance.

travel alone

But you will also learn that home is a state of being. That
you can't care for a withering Chrysanthemum—
or a dying spouse or friend—until you've worn
loss like your Sunday best.

live alone

That you can't, honestly, tell someone, *You'll be okay,*
whatever happens. Until you've squeezed
your broken body through a bus's shattered window—

mourn alone.

across the lifeless body of a woman, you were just
sharing crackers with—bus teetering on a cliff
3,000 feet above sea level, in a country that is no longer yours,
on your way to nowhere.

The Seed

I

When my father—*Baba*—was two, he stuffed a radish seed up his nose.
This was before the war when the scrub-covered foothills of Greece
were ripe for growth.

After a few weeks, a bustle grew that blocked his breathing.
I can see his mother rushing him like a sack of sand to the local doctor—
who, with puckered lips, removes the unlikely garden. His nose for
evermore one wilted bouquet.

When I'm two, I squeeze it like it's a horn, and when he smiles,
it turns into the shape of an upside-down heart. This nose

that traveled across the Atlantic to a country that didn't want it,
without structure, with memories of gun barrels.

II

My son has my Baba's nose—unaltered and intact
like a recreation of the Statue of Zeus at Olympia.
It grows amongst the weeds in the concrete cracks of New York City:
where dreams of freedom are scattered. Where footprints
formed the path to here.

We'll Wrap Up the School Year with Neon Shoes

> *As the last day of school was drawing near, Robb Elementary students*
> *were celebrating with special themed dress days, including Tuesday's*
> *theme of "Footloose and Fancy."*
> —*CNN, May 26, 2022*

and listen to the pledge of allegiance
once more,
and take turns washing our hands
from playing outside.

We'll gather on the familiar carpet of the earth
where Annabelle will sit on North America
and Ellie on Africa
as we've done all year.
Dark-soled shoe stains in the center
where we've left our marks.

We'll pass the vanilla-frosted cupcakes,
Snyder's pretzel sticks and Apple & Eve juice boxes
that our mothers packed with notes of love for our teacher.

For the last time,
we'll speak of Revere, and "Please Excuse My Dear Aunt Sally" and
Hughes' "Dream Variations."
And share plans for the night,
summer . . .
September . . .

as if.

Mom Says, They Must Think I'm Dead Also

My friends are all dying, and their kids don't call to tell me.
Mary always loved you, she says—
Mary, who died in the night's dim hollow. I never thought of her
loving me or not loving me (an orchid left out in the rain).
If I'm honest, haven't thought much of her at all.

But now, I remember them in our old salon—my ten-year old
sweaty thighs cling to the plastic hair-dryer seat.
Mom struggles to free Mary's hair like it's a string
of tangled pearls, while Mary clutches her words—as if
to utter fear of cancer will set it loose.

Strands of her hair cover mom's hands like lace gloves.
Rose-scented conditioner fills the space between us.

He Takes His Children to The Site of His Victim's Remains

> *According to court testimony, Wayne Couzens took his children to play*
> *in the same woods where he had dumped Sarah Everard's body days*
> *earlier.*
> —*Yahoo! News, September 2021*

Lie here among the stripped crocuses,
and cover yourselves with a blanket of light.

Don't venture too far,
you don't know what kind of danger awaits.

I will be right over there, gathering
a basket of frost.

And be quiet as to not wake the blackbirds,
who, only yesterday,

were singing.

A Twenty-Three-Year-Old Dies Opening the Door

Rewind it all:

He doesn't see the other young man—the one with the tattoos on his face—
the one holding that assault rifle, pacing back and forth outside.
We will later see it all on the Ring doorbell footage of the recording studio
we never heard of. A week later, a forty-three-year-old man is gunned down
walking in broad daylight. The man who told us on Facebook, who witnessed
it, just left the liquor store. He said there was blood everywhere like tossed paint.
He was so scared he snuck back into the store, hugging his newly purchased bottle
of New Amsterdam Vodka. The dead man's blood reaching for him like a hand
as he waited for the sirens.

yell to all of them: don't take that walk outside . . .or inside . . .or get that
skull tattoo . . .or make that sweet-talking friend . . .or buy that AK-47 . . .or
that New Amsterdam . . .or take that breath . . .

Do not open that door.

Disappear from Facebook

Don't announce it to the world
like a mistress calling her lover's wife
to say *it's over.*

Don't stand at the pulpit
of pretentiousness patronizing
the sinning congregation in your ripped pantyhose.

Just disappear like Kristy Shi
who took a cab to the Verrazano Bridge,
tipped her driver generously,
then jumped into The Narrows
arms waving as she was wrapped
in the embrace of a gray cotton sweater—
having left no message.

Don't say, *my friends know how to reach me.*

Riding the Bus with My Mother

to Kissena Farms on Fridays.
We pack Granny Smith apples, pink plums
and Heirloom tomatoes into bags
until the plastic expands like a swollen belly.

We move through the aisles without words,
repeating the refrain with Russet potatoes,
string beans and red grapes.
The weight of the wagon overwhelms
my small frame until my mother takes over,
careful to not veer into the children
stealing cherries.

With our doubled-bagged groceries
and stiff necks,
we board the packed Q44 back home.
My tiny right-hand clings to the back
of the bus seat, while two bags hang
from my left like kettlebells.

My spread-out legs stabilize my movements
as my mother leans over—
Women, she whispers,
must learn to carry things.

I nod in acknowledgment as an apple
rolls under my feet.

The Last Day of Summer

She's twelve—
a faux-leather fringed bag
holds her confidence in place.
The tips of her ballet shoes peep out like a Labrador
framed by a partially rolled-down
car window.
Her pigtails swish back and forth
and greet the day.

He's older—
with limbs that have outgrown
their roots
like wild weeds.
His red cap flaps
without saying much.
His Pumas hit the pavement with a groove
as he draws closer.

It's unclear, even years later,
why he pushed her into that well-manicured,
prickly, piercing bush;
tore the bag from her torso
until all that was left
were the bag's fringes—
hanging on the shrub like ornaments
and waving the summer goodbye.

Travel

The traveler sees what he sees.
The tourist sees what he has come to see.
G.K. Chesterton

To the Woman on JetBlue Flight 483 from New York to San Francisco

I saw you take off your blue embroidered shawl,
spaghetti straps exposed your bare, boney shoulders.
You whispered something to my daughter, all I heard,
"It's a nice wrap—wash it."
You were sitting next to her, a few rows behind me and I assumed
you became fast friends—
at eleven-years old,
she still chats with everyone.
But she didn't say much back,
a quiet thank you
as she nodded her head in compliance,
wrapped the shawl around her small waist.
It hung like a hula skirt—
covering her blood-stained pink leggings,
her first cycle ever on this fresh new day.

Before

my father passes away, I hand him a photograph
          of us standing together in front of a bakery
which once housed his father's tailor shop. Now,
          a lavish strawberry cake smiles in the background
as we swelter under Greece's sun—
          sideburns frame his face as I hug my stuffed Snoopy.
It's 1980. In 1942, in this same space, same square of ground,
          a Nazi demands my father, still a child, sew one
Kriegsmarine button onto his uniform jacket. My father's slight fingers
          guide the thread through the needle
like a prisoner squeezing into a narrow hole to escape.
          My grandfather watches without exhaling.
For years, his memories return here: his fisherman cap grazing
          the Nazi's arm as he bows his head
to his bluish-stained fingernails.

The Story

from the same wood-paneled porch,
where we once gathered for
"Happy Days" and "Laverne & Shirley"—
the polypropylene beige carpet holds us up,
the one we couldn't dirty.

Mother listens with plain burnt toast
and black tea in hand. She gathers details,
broken seashells that were once whole, watches.
My brother tells his story
about sexual abuse on the local news:
The name of the teacher we trusted hangs among us.

My brother speaks: details pour out like a hole in a bag of rice,
grains mix with where dust settled until you can't tell the difference
between *what is* and *what was.*

The mug misses her mouth—scalding tea drips down her chin
until it's everywhere.

A Warm February Day in New York

The snowplows trumpet like an elephant stampede down Victory Boulevard.
Two-to-three inches of snow expected tomorrow, but today, we wear short-sleeved
shirts and frayed shorts from last summer—turn off the heat and thank groundhog
Chuck for his early spring prediction.

We consume the day like an inmate's last meal:

      Neighbors spend the day planting carrots, tomatoes, and
cauliflower.

      I move my daughter's neglected dollhouse, keyboard,
guitar to the curb: "Works well. Enjoy." A young
      boy jumps out his dad's Toyota Sienna, grabs the
keyboard and gives me a thumbs up.

      The smell of sweet smoke transports us to a summer
cookout.

      We drive to Brooklyn's Shirley Chisholm State Park,
wildflowers
      on a toxic dump.

On our way home, the sunset drops its pink hue like a crocheted baby's blanket.
The Verrazano Bridge's arches are sculpted in the shape of a woman's breasts.
The deck its ribcage. We follow its breath back home.

Of All the Stories of WWII

that my father told me, the one I remember most begins
with the Nazi's disposing his teenage cousin's body
on the footsteps of his home. I imagine his mother, my father's aunt,
opening the door perhaps with plans to visit her fig tree that day
or having heard a thump opens the door, and there, her son's
contorted body, covered in red like the color of Greek Easter eggs, his body
draped like a tablecloth across the cold cobblestone steps.
I wonder, after the wailing, after the neighbors
are summoned to their windows and perform the sign of the cross
over and over, muttering, "καθάρματα,"—bastards,
did his mother wrap his body in his warm bedroom sheets?
The ones still infused with his sweat, or did she lay in those sheets
for years inhaling him over and over until her tears and his sweat
became one language.

Did she wrap him in an old cloth, perhaps, a muslin she bought?
For a dress she was thinking of making for a παναγυρι—a festival—before
there was war where she would bring her famous Vyssinátha
(sour cherry cordial).

They're all dead now: my father, his aunt, the Nazi. A young couple
lives in that house. Each morning they exhale the night,
and step into the greeting of the enduring fig tree.

Multiple Myeloma

You
took residence in my bones,
pushed out my defenses.
Suppressed the flow of oxygen
like an aging ocean current.
A fortress formed around my heart.

After weeks of chemo,
your eviction leaves space
in the soil of my bones. Bones
collapse like a game of Jenga.

I no longer want to be your marionette.

Let's go back to when I didn't know your name—
when I could walk the woods

alone.

The Mammogram

My x-ray, a map
of gravel sidewalks.
White specks drizzled
amongst the cracked concrete.
Bright white lines like highways
leading to nowhere.
The outline of a seagull
in the posterior outer left chamber.
Only I can see it.

The radiologist's rigid finger like a knife
points to white specks: microcalcifications—
They can be something or nothing.
Cold, monster-like machines
Can detect so much more these days:
aging cells transforming, turning
into what will be.

Glass Ornament

I was a child, after all.

Another Christmas ornament shattered: the silver bell, the last
from the collection my mother meticulously saved and stowed away
for one day. That day has sadly come and gone—

now shards of sparkling glass splattered underneath
the coniferous tree, how I've brushed it all away—

like the immigrant dreams she once carried in her valise,
neatly wrapped for my consumption, gifts
left unopened—

there was no such fragility in my mother's house,
festive trees adorned as perfectly as Grace Kelly.
Mother's hands scrupulously shifting
what I had recklessly placed—

The silver bell mammoth in my dainty hands. Mother's fingers
wrapped around the ornament's hook, a thread bearing the weight
between us.

The Immigrants' Children Grow Up

We grew in the basements of Greek Orthodox churches—St. Demetrios, St.
Nicholas, St. Nectarios . . . The smell of frankincense and rotting eggs. On
     Greek Independence Day,
we pledged allegiance to Poseidon and Ares and boys dressed as Tsolias—
four-hundred pleats to represent the Ottoman occupation.

On Orthodox Good Friday, we led a funeral procession: followed Jesus'
tomb through the streets of Queens, through the aromas of sewage,
petroleum and burnt pizza.

Later, we dyed our eggs blood red, and cracked their tops and bottoms until
one perfect egg remained: a symbol of rebirth and luck.

Summers, we were shipped on TWAs to Greece and ate figs and bathed in
     the Aegean
with our Yiayias and Papous. Our parents needed to send us somewhere
where they belonged. Where we wanted to belong.

Then, we changed our names, dyed our hair blond, moved to the tree-lined
suburbs, into the white house on the cul-de-sac.

Now, on Orthodox Easter, we crack red eggs with other youth soccer
     families in a Cracker Barrel
along Interstate 95; pass the eggs around like forgotten candy. We don't
think about the basements of our youth. Our parents waking at 4am to serve
coffee at diners or alter someone's gown in a dark room in the company of
mice and mothballs.

And we don't think about our old neighbors, who warned their kids about
     us: *Don't they know—*
they're in America now?

Those same neighbors we now crack eggs with.
The ones we've become.

The Feast Day of St. Elias

We wake early
to the smell of minced garlic and onion.
My mother is quiet in her kitchen.
Today, like every year, she will recall
the recipes of her youth.
Recite them like chants.
Prepare for company to commemorate
St. Elias, my father's Name Day.
She will not smile
until the guests arrive.
Sweat will be her veil.
Her hands hard and slippery
from rolling meat.
Phyllo dough
her armor.

Don't Arrive

When you set sail for Ithaca,
wish for the road to be long,
full of adventures, full of knowledge.
C.P. Cavafy

Because I Don't Read Descriptions

—Dedicated to my unborn

I planted corn
instead of cucumbers.
I knew something was wrong,
when angels arrived
with welcome wings.
Their silky-golden hair grew
until my urban driveway
looked like heaven's gate.
Angels with sunburst halo crowns,
yellow spears and seeds wrapped
in wool blankets.

Driving from My Childhood Home on Passover

the familiar warmth of streetlights
set between the London Plane Trees and White Oaks
guide our way to Main Street.

A man appears in the middle of the street
waving his arms like he was jumping jacks
but with stationary legs.

My husband slows and stops
before I can warn him—*keep going.*
These days, you never know:
"Good Samaritan dies . . ."

A thin man rapidly approaches.
I recognize his long side curls, untrimmed beard,
heavy-brimmed hat and long black coat.
He's as familiar as the neighborhood's Bur Oaks.

I roll down the window,
his voice louder than the radio—

a Passover seder
        people gathered
lights turned off
        my children
playing (or was that praying)
        family waiting,
please

Where are the children? I look beyond into the glow of orange lights.

I follow his swift steps
pass the multifamily, semi-attached brick houses,
up a long dark staircase towards murmurs
and aromas of garlic and browned brisket.
I follow a woman's shadow to a wall,
flip the weightless switch as if to cue the audience.
Sounds simmer down.

        Smiles follow me into
        the hollowness of the night

in the direction of laughing children.

First Adult Furniture

One day, we'll revisit this.
You'll hand me a photo of my son
wearing those green paisley rain boots he loved.
Why didn't I hold on to those boots?

A Tibetan hand-painted end table,
a bright face framed in gold
with a permanent smile in the shape
of a shiny brass handle.

We sit on synthetic carpet
surrounded by hissing pipes,
a sunken mattress, empty
deli salad bowls with remnants
of encrusted honey mustard dressing.
You, a blooming lily alongside a ditch.

I was like a child then
given permission to walk alone
to the bodega for the first time.

You now wait for me in our foyer
carry the artifacts of new life:
coffee-stained recital programs,
school photos of my children learning to smile,
tissues transformed into a rose—
a note to mommy.

I deliver these to you
the way a dying spouse hands his wife his ring,
her clenched hand opens like a hibiscus
and then closes.

My Son Grabs the Map

And we're now following him
through the redwood forest, to the ravine,
up the Pacific coast.
I ask him to watch his steps,
but he hikes with urgency like we're late for a funeral.
He's full of newfound wisdom,
almost possessed,
explaining the redwoods are older
than Jesus.
That younger redwoods
draw nutrients and wisdom from the roots of their elders
and once they have passed,
the next generation encircles them
in one final act of reverence.

My Daughter Discovers Her Face

I

She's ten and her skin is perfect and plump
like a fresh bed pillow.

She examines her features in various light
like a forensic scientist looks for evidence.

> I also learned to study the light:
> draw the curtains in and avoid my reflection.

She studies the shape of her eyes and nostrils.
and how they contract and expand when she smiles.

> I want her to not care:
> Frida Kahlo with ebony eyeliner.

She motions for me to sit on the edge
of her bed and raises her mirror.

> I'm mesmerized by our reflections
> like a spirit looking down at the body

and for once seeing it all so clearly.
Am I pretty? she asks no one.

II

When you arrive,
I'm told you're a girl with the most beautiful lashes.

Year one,
unable to walk, you shout for chocolate ice cream.

Year two,
you play peek-a-boo with grandma;
you both laugh as your pajama gown peaks through the chair's legs.
Grandma will pass away in a few weeks.

Year three,
upgraded to first class, the man next to you sighs upon seeing you;
you order a well-done steak, chocolate ice cream and sleep for nine straight hours.

Year four,
you inherit a wardrobe of gowns from family
friends and wear a different one—paired with glitter silver pumps—
to camp all summer.

Year five,
instead of "A is for Apple," you respond, "But, I is for Igloo."

Year six,
a homeless woman offers to buy you ice cream
after you stop to talk with her; you smile
as she follows us into the bodega
asking us for your favorite flavor (chocolate).

Year seven,
you're finally tall enough to ride Animal Kingdom's Primal Whirl roller
    coaster;
you proudly step to the front of the line with your time travel ticket.

Year eight,
you earn your first medal for winning a potato-chip eating contest,
we find crumbs in your hair for days.

Year nine,
(school abruptly ends, the world falls apart)
you tend to Mexican Sunflowers and rosemary,
tape messages of love on our windows
and sign online petitions for justice
in response to George Floyd's death.

On your first day of year ten,
We spend the day at Easton Beach in Newport, Rhode Island.
You move to the ocean's rhythm as it delivers you back to us
over and over.

May it always be so.

Sunday Mourning

This can be anyone's Sunday morning in America
two days before the election.
It's been raining for days.

On my way to get coffee—*medium with a splash of skim*—
I stop at a red light in front of a church.
A wrinkled white man points
his poster at me like a loaded gun:
"Pro-God/Pro-Trump."
He waits for a smile.

Motorcyclists swarm the avenue
like a pack of starving Rottweilers—
push their way in front
of my sleepy suburban SUV.
They release American and MAGA like firecrackers.
Wind whips the fabric around
as if engaged in a group tango.

Confetti drifts like thoughts:
splashes of red, white, and blue
land on my wet windshield,
and absorb the raindrops
like the tears of a crying child
being wiped by his mother.
And, for a moment,
I can see.

Waiting For the Election Results

As we once awaited on news of your father's surgery:
a chestnut-sized tumor pushing
its way against his trachea.
How could something so small be so suffocating?

Volunteers process mail-in votes like surgeons.
A world stands by for the results of this tumor,
which also grew,
as we waved our arms like a new mother
flagging down traffic for help:
a newborn wrapped in blankets—
blue and not breathing.
No one would stop.

We play it all back,
how the tumor grew,
eventually spread like mold
infected all the organs,
blocked the airways.
We wait on a gasp of air.

You'll Get the News

when you're mid-laugh,
or drinking a strawberry

smoothie, or on a hike with friends. When the news
comes, it comes crackled like a radio transmission
from a foreign land. At first, you look away. Glance
over it like another headline on your newsfeed.
If you're out with clients, you'll take another swig
of your chardonnay. Pop another bacon-wrapped scallop
in your mouth, glance at your red-chipped, sweaty fingers.
Inhale one last moment of oblivion before you read

the message again, and again...
Your heart, a countdown clock.

When it comes, it'll interrupt the mundane, change you,
tragedy knocking the door down at dinner time—the news,
it'll startle you into consciousness. You'll get that, the woman
laughing a few seconds earlier, you'll come to hate her.

His Voice Was the First to Go

I owe you a response.

Every other syllable needed to be saved
from cancer's chokehold.
I filled in for what was left unsaid.

Father's voice was hoarse before
the cancer took hold. Raspy from years of church
chanting, conversations about politics, terrorism . . .
invasions. Even if twenty-five years have passed,
even if you're dead. I've measured these misgivings
in milliliters. I'm middle-aged and have my own questions,
resented that even in death, you were afraid to be seen.
I heard you, even if I couldn't look at you—bald, blind,

I sank into the silence of death. Replayed it over
and over, turned up the volume, but still
couldn't hear. I couldn't look at your urine-colored,
dying skin, wore my headphones on mute, sat cross armed
by your hospital bed—listened to the shallow breaths,
and vitals as if we had time. Today,

I found your professional dressmaker scissors: the pair
your father gave you, the ones that dressed the community
we hid from,
the ones that bought the Dutch Colonial we lived in.
For all to see, I will soon frame them.

Tell me, are the cut, disjointed sound bites of our lives
what makes the bloodthirsty melody come alive?
We walked a mile to take the city bus,
far from where the congregation would see us
without a car, that life of pride, pressed shirt, and tie
worn to the market. One day, he whispered:

You must hate me.

Snow Day

Irene's cheeks are flushed
like a baby's tush.
A wool scarf frames her face,
a bow tied at her hairline.
Happiness holds the day together.

The aroma of maple syrup and bacon permeates the house,
The fireplace revs up its engine.
The radiator welcomes the wet wool hats.

She builds a snowman:
two sticks for eyes, a lop-sided Twizzler for the mouth
She wraps her scarf around his belly
to keep him safe.

Snowflakes disappear by the nape of her neck
as we clear a path to nowhere.